"Bring The Classics To Life"

From the Earth to the Moon

LEVEL 4

Series Designer
Philip J. Solimene

Editor
Laura Solimene

EDCON

Long Island, New York

Story Adaptor
Kim Cory

Author
Jules Verne

About the Author

Jules Verne, (1828-1905), was a French writer who wrote some of the first science fiction stories. Amazingly, he wrote about airplanes, submarines, and television, long before any of these were invented. In his book, *From the Earth to the Moon*, written in 1865, Jules Verne wrote about space travel and Man's journey to the moon. Yet Man did not step foot on the moon's surface until the year 1969, more than 100 years later.

Copyright © 1995
A/V Concepts Corp.
Long Island, New York

Printed in U.S.A.
ISBN# 1-55576-181-X

CONTENTS

Words Used 4, 5

NO.	TITTLE	SYNOPSIS	PAGE
61	**The Gun Club**	The Gun Club is formed during the time of the Civil War.	6
62	**The Plan**	The Gun Club makes plans to build a cannon that could send something to the moon.	12
63	**The October Meeting**	Impey Barbicane chooses a committee to help him carry out his plan.	18
64	**The Bet**	Captain Nicholl demands that the government stop Barbicane's plan. He bets Barbicane $15,000.00 that his plan will never work.	24
65	**Off To Florida**	The Committee sets out to choose the right spot for the launch.	30
66	**A Message To Barbicane**	Michel Ardan volunteers to go to the moon in the cannon's shell.	36
67	**Michel Ardan Arrives**	Michel Ardan comes to America to meet Barbicane, and tell the world of his plan to go to the moon.	42
68	**The Quarrel**	Captain Nicholl, longtime enemy of Impey Barbicane, challenges him to a duel.	48
69	**Ready to Go**	Final preparations are made for the approaching launch.	54
70	**Ready! Set! Fire!**	On a cool, sunny day in December, the astronauts make their way into space.	60

WORDS USED

Story 61	Story 62	Story 63	Story 64	Story 65
KEY WORDS				
action	celebrate	chosen	bet	alligator
colonel	distant	design	demand	arrangement
insist	national	October	expensive	climate
period	planet	problem	immediately	degree
succeed	preparation	rocket	length	tropical
weary	pride	support	powder	zero
NECESSARY WORDS				
bored	astronomer	aluminum	alloy	latitude
communicating	bruised	axis	armor	malaria
energy	equator	committee	coarse	project
firearms	launch	gravity	grudge	
hippopotamuses	observatory	magnification	rival	
members	parallel		ton	
snoring	telegraph			
thrilling				
weapons				
Yankee				

WORDS USED

Story 66	Story 67	Story 68	Story 69	Story 70
KEY WORDS				
accept	accent	fact	astronaut	nuisance
date	artist	gentleman	check	orbit
December	champion	honesty	guest	solve
disgrace	crazy	hotel	locate	spent
examination	flight	mention	overhead	upset
impatient	news	quarrel	praise	urge
NECESSARY WORDS				
cablegram	anchor	challenged	capsule	anthem
comment	cell	duel	chemical	countdown
congratulated	intelligent	enemy	entrance	gravity
platform	port	platform	include	meteor
toast	risk		knights	national
volcano			portholes	switch

The Gun Club

PREPARATION

Key Words

action	(ak´shən)	the doing of something *Beth took quick <u>action</u> when her brother was hurt.*
colonel	(kėr´nl)	a military officer *She wanted to become a <u>colonel</u> in the Army.*
insist	(in sist´)	to demand strongly *"I <u>insist</u> you eat all your green vegetables!" his mother said.*
period	(pir´ē əd)	an amount of time that goes by *Paul couldn't play in the second <u>period</u> of the hockey game.*
succeed	(sek sēd´)	to manage to do what was planned *We will <u>succeed</u> in planting our vegetable garden this weekend.*
weary	(wir´ē)	tired; having little or no interest left; bored *They were <u>weary</u> of watching T.V. by the 6th rainy day.*

The Gun Club

Necessary Words

bored	(bôrd)	not interested in something *Katie was <u>bored</u> with her school work.*
communicating	(kə mū´nə kāt ing)	a means to exchange information *Do you believe those cats are <u>communicating</u> with each other?*
energy	(en´ər jē)	strength or power to work or be active *Gina has so much <u>energy</u> today.*
firearms	(fīr´ärms´)	rifles, pistols, or other weapons that shoot bullets or shells and are small enough to carry *It is against the law to bring <u>firearms</u> to school.*
hippopotamuses	(hip´ə pot´ə mes əs)	large animals with a thick skin and short legs. They feed on plants and live in or near rivers in Africa. *Can <u>hippopotamuses</u> breathe under water?*
members	(mem´bərs)	any one of the persons who make up a club *The new Bike Club has 33 <u>members</u> in all.*
snoring	(snôr´ing)	to breathe with rough sounds while one sleeps *I wish my sister would stop <u>snoring</u>.*
thrilling	(thril´ing)	to feel or make very excited *That ride on the new roller coaster was quite <u>thrilling</u>.*
weapons	(wep´əns)	things used in fighting, such as guns *Our mother thought our toy guns looked like real <u>weapons</u>.*
Yankee	(yang´kē)	a person born or living in the northern part of the United States, especially New England *During the Civil War, a Southener would not be seen with a <u>Yankee</u>.*

People

Colonel Bloomsberry   is an important member of the Gun Club.

Places

Baltimore   is a seaport in northern Maryland.

England   is the south part of the island of Great Britain.

Europe   is the continent between Asia and the Atlantic Ocean.

The Gun Club

The American members of the Gun Club worked hard to build a huge cannon.

Preview: 1. Read the name of the story.
2. Look at the picture.
3. Read the sentence under the picture.
4. Read the first paragraph of the story.
5. Then answer the following question.

You learned from your preview that the Civil War was fought between
___a. the North and the South.
___b. the East and the West.
___c. the South and the West.
___d. the East and the North.

Turn to the Comprehension Check on page 10 for the right answer.

Now read the story.

Read to find out about Impey Barbicane's plan.

The Gun Club

A long time ago there was a war between the North and the South. This period of time was called the Civil War. People left their work and homes. They wanted to be soldiers and captains. A lot of money was spent on war supplies. During the Civil War an important club was formed.

The newspapers ran many stories about the thrilling new guns and cannons being made. Sometimes one american has an idea. He looks for other Americans who share his idea. Three people may share an idea. So they choose a president. Then two vice presidents. Soon their club is started. This is how it happened in Baltimore. A man invented a new cannon. Then he joined with a man who molded it. Next, they joined with another man who fired it. A month after it was formed, the Gun Club had a total of 30,575 members in different places.

There was one rule of the Club. The men joining must have invented a cannon or some other kind of gun. The American members made a huge cannon. This cannon shot farther than any cannon had before. With each of its shots, soldiers fell. This cannon was the idea of J.T. Maston. He was the secretary of the Gun Club. His idea was a huge success.

The Gun Club was made up of very nice men. Some of these Gun Club members were officers. Many came back from the war without arms or legs. Then, one day, the shooting slowed down. The war was coming to an end. Then it stopped. Members of the gun Club became very bored. The rooms of their club became empty. Sounds of snoring came from dark corners.

"It's disappointing!" Tom Hunter said one evening. "There's nothing to do! What a weary life!"

"You're right!" spoke Colonel Bloomsberry.

"And no war in sight!" said J.T. Maston. He scratched his head with the hook at the end of his arm. "And only this morning I made a set of plans that will change how wars work!"

"How interesting!" said Tom Hunter. "Maybe we could build weapons for the wars taking place in Europe."

"No," said Maston, "That wouldn't work. It seems that Americans don't want to take action! For example, didn't America once belong to England?"

"Yes," answered Tom.

"Then why shouldn't it be England's turn to belong to America?" said Maston.

The club members argued for a long time. It seemed that the Club might break up.

But the very next day, each member of the club received the following message:

Baltimore, October 3

The president of the Gun Club has the honor of telling his friends that during the meeting on October 5, he will make an announcement that they will be very interested in. He insists they all be at the meeting.

Imprey Barbicane
President

October 5 came. All the members crowded into a hall. It was a big meeting. Models of cannons, rifles and other war weapons filled the hall. A huge iron desk was at the far end of the room. Behind it sat the president of the Club, Impey Barbicane. The club members knew he would not have insisted they be there unless it was very important.

Impey Barbicane was a quiet, cold, serious man. A true Yankee. He had made a fortune in the lumber business. He stood out from the other men. Barbicane was one of the lucky men who still had all his arms and legs.

The clock struck 8. Everyone was quiet.

"My friends, we have been at peace for too long a period! We must take action! Any war that would bring back the use of weapons would be welcome!" spoke Barbicane.

The members yelled in support.

Barbicane continued. "But for now, war is not possible. We must accept this and find another way to use our energy. For a long time I have been thinking of a plan,. This plan will make a great noise in the world."

"A great noise?" the Colonel asked with excitement.

"You have all seen the moon, haven't you?" Barbicane asked. "Well, I will lead you weary men on an adventure. An adventure to the moon! We know a great deal about it. But so far, no one has been able to succeed in communicating with it. People from ages ago have told of seeing people on the moon. In 1835, one scientist, looking at the moon through a telescope, told of seeing caves with hippopotamuses living in them!"

The crowd cheered! Each member of the Club was excited by Barbicane's words.

"Silence!" they shouted from all over the hall.

The voices died down. Barbicane spoke again, this time in a deeper voice. "You all know how firearms have improved these last few years. With this in mind, I started to wonder if it would be possible to build a huge cannon. A cannon large enough to shoot something to the moon."

"Oh!" the crowd gasped.

"I have looked at it carefully," Barbicane said. "And I think we can succeed! And so my good friends, let's do it!"

The Gun Club

COMPREHENSION CHECK

Choose the best answer.

1. The Gun Club was formed in the city of
   _____a. Biltmore.
   _____b. Baltimore.
   _____c. Bridgewater.
   _____d. Brighton.

2. After one month, the Gun Club had
   _____a. 3,000 members.
   _____b. more than 30,000 members.
   _____c. more than 70,000 members.
   _____d. more than one million members.

3. To become a member of the Club, a person must have invented some kind of
   _____a. animal trap.
   _____b. special knife.
   _____c. hammer or spoon.
   _____d. cannon or gun.

4. J.T. Maston, the secretary of the Gun Club, had an idea to build
   _____a. a huge cannon.
   _____b. a quiet cannon.
   _____c. a safe cannon.
   _____d. a famous cannon.

5. When the war ended, the members of the Gun Club became
   _____a. sick.
   _____b. amused.
   _____c. bored.
   _____d. happy.

6. The members of the Gun Club seemed to like the idea of war because
   _____a. they all loved the fighting.
   _____b. it kept them away from home.
   _____c. it gave them all something to talk about.
   _____d. it gave them a reason to continue making weapons.

7. Just as the Club seemed as if it would break up,
   _____a. Impey Barbicane came up with a new idea to keep the members busy.
   _____b. Impey Barbicane became sick.
   _____c. Impey Barbicane left for England.
   _____d. Impey Barbicane made a great noise in the world.

8. Impey Barbicane was
   _____a. the Club's president.
   _____b. the Club's vice president.
   _____c. the Club's secretary.
   _____d. the Club's enemy.

9. Another name for this story could be
   _____a. "Sharing Ideas."
   _____b. "Life During the Civil War."
   _____c. "Mr. Barbicane Calls a Meeting."
   _____d. "Adventure to the Moon!"

10. This story is mainly about
   _____a. men who build cannons.
   _____b. a club that was formed during the time of the Civil War.
   _____c. a man who made a fortune in the lumber business.
   _____d. why the members of the Gun Club became bored.

Check your answers with the key on page 67.

This page may be reproduced for classroom use.

The Gun Club

VOCABULARY CHECK

action	colonel	insist	period	succeed	weary

I. Sentences to Finish
Fill in the blank in each sentence with the correct key word from the box above.

1. The _____ has been in the Army for ten years.

2. "I _____ that you get plenty of rest," said the doctor.

3. I know that Doug will _____ in life, for he works hard.

4. The _____ soldiers stopped to rest.

5. One day is a _____ of twenty-four hours.

6. Bill took quick _____ to save the boy from drowning.

II. Matching
Write the letter of the correct meaning from Column B next to the key word in Column A.

Column A

_____1. action
_____2. colonel
_____3. insist
_____4. period
_____5. succeed
_____6. weary

Column B

a. to manage to do what was planned
b. a portion of time that goes by
c. the doing of something
d. a military officer
e. tired; having little or no interest left; bored
f. to demand strongly

Check your answers with the key on page 69.

This page may be reproduced for classroom use.

The Plan

PREPARATION

Key Words

celebrate	(sel´ə brāt)	to honor a special day or event with a party or other activity *Amy loved to <u>celebrate</u> her birthday with cake and presents.*
distant	(dis´tənt)	far away in space or time *Kindergarten was a <u>distant</u> memory for Pat now that she was in 4th grade.*
national	(nash´ən l)	having to do with a nation as a whole *The runner became a <u>national</u> hero when she won the gold medal.*
planet	(plan´it)	any of the large bodies that revolve around the sun *The closest <u>planet</u> to the sun is Mercury.*
preparation	(prep´ə rā¯shən)	the act of getting ready *The class spent a great deal of time in <u>preparation</u> for their play.*
pride	(prīd)	pleasure or satisfaction from doing something *Amanda took great <u>pride</u> in her strong math skills.*

The Plan

Necessary Words

astronomer   (əs tron´ə mər)   a scientist who studies the motion, size and makeup of the stars, planets, comets, and other things found in space
The famous <u>astronomer</u> had a new planet named after him.

bruised   (brüzed)   to hurt the outside of skin causing it to darken in color
He <u>bruised</u> the skin of the peach when he dropped it.

equator   (i kwā´t ər)   an imaginary circle around the middle of the earth halfway between the North and the South Poles
The United States is north of the <u>equator</u>.

launch   (lônch)   to throw, hurl, or send off with some force
The team will <u>launch</u> the spaceship on Saturday.

observatory   (əb zёr´və tô´rē)   a building with telescopes and other equipment in it for studying the sun, moon, stars, planets, and weather
The <u>observatory</u> was opened for public viewing of the stars.

parallel   (par´ə lel)   any one of the imaginary circles around the earth that are parallel to the equator and that mark degrees of latitude
Paul had to learn that the equator was 0 <u>parallel</u> on the map.

telegraph   (tel´ə graf)   a means for sending messages by electricity
We sent Mother a message by <u>telegraph</u> to let her know we were coming.

Places

Cambridge   is a city in the state of Massachusetts.

The Plan

Barbicane's idea caused a great wave of excitement!

Preview: 1. Read the name of the story.
2. Look at the picture.
3. Read the sentence under the picture.
4. Read the first paragraph of the story.
5. Then answer the following question.

You learned from your preview that Barbicane's idea was to build a cannon that would

___a. reach the sun.
___b. reach the moon.
___c. travel through space.
___d. make the earth tremble.

Turn to the Comprehension Check on page 16 for the right answer.

Now read the story.

Read to find out if Barbicane's idea is possible.

The Plan

The last few words Barbicane spoke to the members of the Gun Club made everyone cheer. "Hurray," they yelled. The idea of building a cannon that could send something to the moon caused a great wave of excitement. Men stomped their feet and clapped their hands. The noise was as loud as several cannons being fired!

Barbicane stayed calm during all this noise. He was lifted onto the shoulders of several men, then carried around as they began to celebrate his words.

Then a strange thing happened. The moon came out and started to shine. It was as if it were celebrating too! Some people waved to it, while others stared at it through telescopes. They acted as if they owned the moon.

Finally, it was 2 o'clock in the morning. People calmed down. Barbicane went home. He was tired and a bit bruised. It had been a national celebration. The railroads had carried the news to all parts of the United States. All the great cities knew about the plan. The same night Barbicane announced his plan, the telegraph wires sent messages to distant places around the country. The whole country swelled with pride.

The next day, over 1500 newspapers carried news of the plan. People wondered if the moon was a complete planet; if it was changing at all. Was it like the earth had been before people lived there? What did the side that couldn't be seen from the earth look like? All that had been planned so far was to send something to the moon. Every newspaper saw this as a start of many experiments. They hoped someday the earth would unlock the last secrets of the moon's world.

Newspapers carried good news about the plan. Many important science groups sent letters of praise to the Gun Club. All were sure the plan would work. Those who didn't believe in it were laughed at. People who made fun of it were in danger. And so Barbicane became a national hero.

Next, preparation began for the big event. First, Barbicane called members of the Gun Club together. They agreed to talk with some astronomers. Together, they worked out the finishing touches of the plan.

There were many questions. The Gun Club mailed a letter to the famous observatory at Cambridge, Massachusetts. The astronomers and scientists there were known around the world. They also had a very powerful telescope. Two days later, the Gun Club received their answer.

CAMBRIDGE, October 7

Mr. Impey Barbicane
President of the Gun Club
Baltimore, Maryland
Dear Mr. Barbicane,

After receiving your letter, our staff met right away. We answered your questions the best we could. Your questions were these:
1. Is it possible to send something to the moon?
2. Exactly how distant is the moon from our earth?
3. How long will what we send be in flight? And when must it be sent to hit the moon in a certain spot?
4. When is the moon in the best position to be reached?
5. At what part of the sky should the cannon be aimed?
6. What will be the position of the moon when the cannon is fired?

Let me answer your *first* question. Yes, it is possible to send something from our planet to the moon.

Now, about the *second* question. Sometimes the moon is close to the earth. Sometimes it is not. So you must figure out the distance from the moon to the earth, carefully.

Now let me answer your *third* question. If something is launched with enough force, how long will it be in flight? It will take 97 hours, 13 minutes and 20 seconds to cover the distance to the moon.

You had a *fourth* question: When would the moon be in the best position for the launching from earth? We have figured out that date. This will be December 1st of next year. It will have to be at midnight. This is the exact time when the moon will be the closest to the earth.

Now, about your *fifth* question. You asked where the cannon should be aimed in the sky. The answer is that it must be somewhere between the equator and the twenty-eighth parallel. This could be either north or south.

Question number *six* asked about the position of the moon. The moon must be at an angle of about 64 degrees when launched.

The members of the Gun club must start preparation right away for the launch. If you miss the date, you will not find the moon in the same spot again for eighteen more years!

We at the observatory are ready to help you if you have any more questions. We wish you well. You are all the pride of America!

Sincerely,
J.M. Belfast
Director

The Plan

COMPREHENSION CHECK

Choose the best answer.

1. Barbicane's idea caused
   _____a. the Gun Club to break up.
   _____b. fighting among the members.
   _____c. a great wave of excitement.
   _____d. little interest among the members.

2. During the celebration, what strange thing happened?
   _____a. The sun came out and started to shine.
   _____b. The moon came out and started to shine.
   _____c. It started to rain very hard.
   _____d. It began to snow.

3. The meeting ended
   _____a. at noon.
   _____b. around 5 o'clock in the morning.
   _____c. around 2 o'clock in the morning.
   _____d. during lunch.

4. Word of Barbicane's idea was carried to all parts of the United States by
   _____a. railroad.
   _____b. telegraph.
   _____c. newspapers.
   _____d. all of the above.

5. People all over the country
   _____a. knew little about the moon.
   _____b. knew all there was to know about the moon.
   _____c. had little interest in the moon.
   _____d. were afraid to learn about the moon.

6. First, Barbicane called the members of the Gun Club together to prepare for the big event. Next, the members talked with some astronomers. Then,
   _____a. Barbicane gave up on his idea.
   _____b. the Gun Club mailed a letter to the observatory at Cambridge.
   _____c. the Gun Club received a letter from the observatory at Cambridge.
   _____d. they aimed their cannon in the sky.

7. How many questions did the Gun Club ask in their letter to the observatory?
   _____a. Three
   _____b. Thirty
   _____c. Sixty
   _____d. Six

8. In their letter, the observatory warned the Gun Club that they must
   _____a. give up their idea.
   _____b. begin preparing for the launch right away.
   _____c. put off their launch for eighteen more years.
   _____d. stop celebrating so much.

9. Another name for this story could be
   _____a. "The Launch."
   _____b. "Barbicane, A National Hero."
   _____c. "Getting Started."
   _____d. "Secrets of the Moon's World."

10. This story is mainly about
   _____a. how the Gun Club worked to make their idea really happen.
   _____b. how to write a letter to an observatory.
   _____c. how to look through a telescope.
   _____d. how a nation celebrated.

Check your answers with the key on page 67.

This page may be reproduced for classroom use.

The Plan

VOCABULARY CHECK

celebrate	distant	national	planet	preparation	pride

I. Sentences to Finish

Fill in the blank in each sentence with the correct key word from the box above.

1. Elizabeth Vaz will _____ her birthday on September 3rd.

2. David took great _____ in cleaning his new car.

3. Our class spent many days working in _____ for the school play.

4. July 4th is a _____ holiday.

5. My days as a young child have become a _____ memory.

6. The _____ Mars is the fourth in order from the sun.

II. Crossword Puzzle

Fill in the puzzle with the key words from the box above. Use the meanings below to help you choose the right word.

ACROSS
1. pleasure or satisfaction from doing something
2. any of the large bodies that revolve around the sun
3. having to do with a nation as a whole

DOWN
1. the act of getting ready
2. far away in space or time
3. to honor a special day or event with a party or some other activity

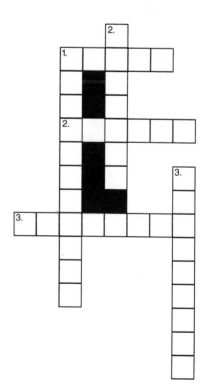

Check your answers with the key on page 69.

This page may be reproduced for classroom use.

The October Meeting

PREPARATION

Key Words

chosen   (chō´zn)   picked out
> *I have <u>chosen</u> Meg as a member of my team.*

design   (di zīn´)   to think up and draw plans for something
> *Jane helped <u>design</u> the cover for the yearbook.*

October   (ok tō´bər)   the tenth month of the year
> *We celebrate Halloween in <u>October</u>.*

problem   (prob´ləm)   a condition, person, or thing that is difficult to deal with or hard to understand
> *Walking through 6 feet of snow in the winter is a real <u>problem</u>.*

rocket   (rok´it)   a long narrow device that is used as a weapon or provides the power for spacecraft
> *Michael's toy <u>rocket</u> shot 20 feet into the air!*

support   (sə pôrt´)   1. hold up
> *Dad used a jack to <u>support</u> the car while he changed the tire.*

2. be in favor of
> *Peg's sister said she would <u>support</u> Peg's idea to go skating.*

The October Meeting

Necessary Words

aluminum (ə lü´mə nəm) a sliver-white, very light metal
Paul took all the <u>aluminum</u> cans back to the store.

axis (ak´sis) the real or imaginary straight line about which a
thing turns
*Mrs. Todd's 4th grade class mapped the earth's <u>axis</u>
for their science project.*

committee (kə mit´ē) a group of persons chosen to do some special thing
The book <u>committee</u> meets every Tuesday evening.

gravity (grav´ə tē) the natural force that draws objects toward the center of
the earth. Gravity causes objects to have weight.
*The astronaut floated in space because there was
no <u>gravity</u>.*

magnification (mag´nə fi cā´shən) the act of making something look larger than it really is
*The <u>magnification</u> of the ant through the
magnifying glass made the ant look like a monster.*

Things

cast iron is a very strong molded (cast) iron.

comet a frozen mass of dust and gas that moves through space. When it passes
near the sun, it becomes a bright ball with a fiery tail.

The October Meeting

Newspapers ran stories about the moon every day.

> **Preview:** 1. Read the name of the story.
> 2. Look at the picture.
> 3. Read the sentence under the picture.
> 4. Read the first two paragraphs of the story.
> 5. Then answer the following question.
>
> You learned from your preview that the distance from the earth to the moon is about
>
> ___a. 234,000 miles.
> ___b. 500,000 miles.
> ___c. 700,000 miles.
> ___d. three million miles.
>
> *Turn to the Comprehension Check on page 22 for the right answer.*

Now read the story.

Read about some of the problems to be worked out before anything could be sent to the moon.

The October Meeting

The moon had been around for a long time. But people acted as if it were brand-new. It took its place among the "stars." Newspapers ran stories about the moon every day. The whole country had "moon fever."

Until this time, most people did not know the distance from the earth to the moon. Now, scientists told them. The average distance was 234,347 miles.

Some people did not understand that the same side of the moon is always seen from the earth. This is because the moon turns once on its axis when circling the earth. They were told, "Go into your dining room. Walk around the table. Always look at its center. When you have walked all the way around it, you will have turned once on your own axis. Pretend the room is the sky. And the table is the earth. Think that you're the moon!" This helped people to understand more clearly.

Some people believed that the moon was once a comet. A few people believed the moon had passed too closely to earth and had been caught by our gravity. Others believed the moon was coming closer every time it went around the earth. They thought it would one day fall against the earth. Finally, people read enough to know that they were wrong.

Impey Barbicane chose a committee from the members to help him carry out his plan. These members were as follows: Barbicane himself, General Morgan, Major Elphiston, and J.T. Maston. On October 8 they met at Barbicane's house. He spoke first.

"Gentlemen, we must clear up an important problem. We must first think about what kind of rocket our cannon will send to the moon."

"Yes," remarked General Morgan.

"Just think what it will be like. We will fire an object at a speed of seven miles a second! But first we must think! We must give an object a speed of 36,000 feet a second. And

we must examine the speeds that have been reached so far. General Morgan can help us with this."

"Yes, I was on the Experiment committee during the war," said the general. "One kind of shell had a range of three miles. It traveled at 1,500 feet every second. Another cannon shot a shell six miles. Its speed was 2,400 miles every second."

"So, 2,400 feet each second is the fastest speed reached so far?" asked Barbicane.

"Yes sir," answered Morgan.

"Then," spoke Barbicane, "let's take the speed of 2,400 feet each second as our starting point. We'll need to increase it times 15. But first let's talk about the design of the rocket itself."

"What about it?" asked Major Elphiston.

Maston answered, "It must be very large; large enough for whoever lives on the moon to notice."

"Yes," said Barbicane. "And also for another important reason."

"What do you mean?" asked the major.

"I mean, it is not enough to send off a rocket and then forget about it. We must be able to watch it until it reaches the moon."

"What!" yelled the general and the major. "Then you must be planning on making the rocket huge!"

"No," spoke Barbicane, "we'll place a telescope on a high mountain and bring magnification to 48,000. That will bring the moon to within five miles. We will be able to see objects only 9 feet wide."

"Wonderful!" cried J.T. Maston.

"Now, what metal have you chosen for the rocket?" asked the major.

"Regular cast iron," replied Barbicane.

"Cast iron? But a cast iron rocket 9 feet wide will be too heavy!" said the general.

"If," said Barbicane, "it is solid. But not if it's hollow."

"Hollow!" they all yelled in surprise.

"So we can put messages in it," explained Barbicane. "But it must be able to support itself - it must weigh 20,000 pounds."

"How thick must the walls be designed?" asked the major.

Barbicane answered, "Here's our problem. How thick must the walls of a cast iron rocket be if it weighs 20,000 pounds? Mr. Maston is our skilled math person. Could you tell us sir?"

"I'll be glad to," he said.

Maston wrote several numbers down on a sheet of paper. Then he said, "The walls would only have to be two inches thick."

"Would that be enough?" asked the major.

"Of course not," said Barbicane.

"Should we use copper instead?" asked Major Elphiston.

"No," spoke Barbicane. "that's also too heavy, so let's choose something better."

"What?" asked Maston.

"How about aluminum," said Barbicane.

"But isn't that expensive?" asked the major.

"It used to be, but now it's down to only $9.00 a pound," answered Barbicane.

"But $9.00 a pound!" said the major. "That's still expensive!"

"Yes," said Barbicane, "but we can do it."

"How much will the rocket weigh?" asked Morgan.

Barbicane had already figured that one out. "Made of aluminum, it will weigh only 19,250 pounds."

"Wonderful!" said Maston, with excitement.

"Fantastic!" added the major. "But at $9.00 a pound, that means it will cost..."

"It will cost $173,250," Barbicane finished. "But we will get plenty of money to support our plan."

"Great!" the committee shouted.

J.T. Maston was pleased at sending an aluminum rocket to the moon. He thought of life there.

This ended the October meeting of the committee.

The October Meeting

COMPREHENSION CHECK

Choose the best answer.

1. People who had "moon fever"
   _____a. were very sick people.
   _____b. were afraid of the moon.
   _____c. were very interested and excited about the moon.
   _____d. had no interest in the moon at all.

2. Some people thought that the moon was once
   _____a. an axis.
   _____b. alive.
   _____c. a comet.
   _____d. a clock.

3. President Barbicane chose a committee
   _____a. to help him carry out his plan.
   _____b. to help raise money for this plan.
   _____c. to help keep his plan a secret from the world.
   _____d. to help him manage the Gun Club.

4. The first committee meeting was held
   _____a. at Maston's house.
   _____b. at the Major's house.
   _____c. at General Morgan's house.
   _____d. at Impey Barbicane's house.

5. What was the main subject of this first meeting?
   _____a. The rocket's design
   _____b. The rocket's speed
   _____c. The cost to build the rocket
   _____d. The rocket's size

6. Barbicane's plan was to watch the rocket's flight to the moon
   _____a. by wearing special glasses.
   _____b. by looking through a magnifying glass.
   _____c. by climbing the tallest mountain.
   _____d. by looking through a telescope.

7. The general felt that the use of cast iron for the rocket's metal would make it
   _____a. too expensive.
   _____b. too heavy.
   _____c. too strong.
   _____d. too stiff.

8. It was decided that the rocket would be made of aluminum. Aluminum was selling for
   _____a. $90.00 per pound.
   _____b. $99.00 per pound.
   _____c. $9.00 per pound.
   _____d. $5.00 per pound.

9. Another name for this story could be
   _____a. "A Problem of Design."
   _____b. "How To Choose a Committee."
   _____c. "Heavy Metal."
   _____d. "Rocket To Nowhere."

10. This story is mainly about
    _____a. the high cost of aluminum.
    _____b. how to use a telescope.
    _____c. a plan that would not work.
    _____d. a group of people getting together to help make an idea work.

Check your answers with the key on page 67.

This page may be reproduced for classroom use.

The October Meeting

VOCABULARY CHECK

chosen	design	October	problem	rocket	support

I. Sentences to Finish

Fill in the blank in each sentence with the correct key word from the box above.

1. Mary had a _____ finding her car keys.

2. We pick pumpkins in _____ and bake pumpkin pie.

3. The _____ will blast off at 11:00 Saturday morning.

4. The table cannot _____ the weight of that heavy lamp.

5. Lisa has been _____ to enter the beauty contest.

6. Bob asked Joe if he would help him _____ his dream car.

II. Using the Words

On the lines below, write six of your own sentences using the key words from the box above. Use each word once, drawing a line under the key word.

1. _____

2. _____

3. _____

4. _____

5. _____

6. _____

Check your answers with the key on page 69.

The Bet

PREPARATION

Key Words

bet	(bet)	a promise to give money or a certain thing to another if he is right and you are wrong *Andy had to pay Stan $1.00 because he lost the <u>bet</u>.*
demand	(d i mand´)	to ask for as a right; ask for with authority *Pete will <u>demand</u> to have his way.*
expensive	(eks pen´siv)	having a high price; costing much *That new sports car had an <u>expensive</u> price tag on it!*
immediately	(i mē´dē it lē)	without delay; at once; right away *Take that wounded boy to the nurse <u>immediately</u>!*
length	(length)	the measure of how long a thing is; the distance from one end to the other end *Carla needed to check the <u>length</u> of the skirt before she bought it.*
powder	(pou´dər)	a substance that's reduced to dust by crushing or grinding; gunpowder *The soldiers loaded the cannon with <u>powder</u>, lit the fuse, then stood back.*

The Bet

Necessary Words

alloy   (al´oi)   a cheap metal that is mixed with a more expensive metal; a mixture of two or more metals
> *The scientist told Paul that bronze is an <u>alloy</u> of copper and tin.*

armor   (är´mər)   covering worn to protect the body in fighting
> *Knights in days of old wore suits of <u>armor</u> to protect themselves in battle.*

coarse   (kôrs)   made up of rather large parts; not fine
> *As the waves lapped over the beach, the <u>coarse</u> sand became smoother.*

grudge   (gruj)   a bad feeling against a person because of something
> *Kathy held a <u>grudge</u> against her sister for telling lies about her.*

rival   (rī´vl)   a person who tries to equal or do better than another
> *They were <u>rivals</u> for first prize at the County Fair pie-eating contest.*

ton   (tun)   a measure of weight that is equal to 2,000 pounds in the U.S. and Canada, and 2,240 pounds in Great Britain
> *Amy knew Beth was stretching the truth when she said her books weighed a <u>ton</u>!*

The Bet

At their next meeting, the committee members work late into the night.

Preview: 1. Read the name of the story.
2. Look at the picture.
3. Read the sentence under the picture.
4. Read the first four paragraphs of the story.
5. Then answer the following question.

You learned from your preview that the most difficult problem the members faced in building the cannon was

___a. its color.
___b. its shape.
___c. its size.
___d. its beauty.

Turn to the Comprehension Check on page 28 for the right answer.

Now read the story.

Read to find out who takes Captain Nicholl's bet.

The Bet

The night after the first meeting, the committee met again. They ate mountains of sandwiches. They drank gallons of tea. Immediately after filling up with food, they talked about their plan.

"Gentlemen," said Barbicane, "we must decide on many questions. What is the length of the *cannon* to be? What shape should it be? What materials should it be built with? And what about its weight?"

"Isn't size the biggest difficulty?" asked the major.

"Yes, it is," answered Barbicane. "But we'll overcome it. A lot depends upon its length and weight. We can make the cannon as strong as we like. It won't have to be moved."

"I think we should make the cannon at least half a mile long!" said Maston.

"Half a mile!" shouted the major and the general, together.

"Yes, half a mile," Maston repeated. "And it still won't be long enough!"

"Come, Maston," said Morgan, "that's too long!"

"Calm down my friends," added Barbicane. "Let's reason. Consider the weight of the rocket being shot. It will weigh 20,000 pounds and it will be only 225 feet long. The cannon would only have to weigh 4,800,000 pounds."

"That's silly!" said Maston. "We might as well use a pistol!"

"I think so too," replied Barbicane. "That's why I think we should times the rocket's length by four. That would make the cannon nine hundred feet long."

After arguing the numbers for a while, they all agreed.

"How thick should we make the cannon's walls?" asked the major.

"Six feet," answered Barbicane.

"It would be grand!" spoke Maston, with excitement.

"I'm thinking of building the cannon into the ground," said Barbicane. "The earth around it will give it strength during the blast."

"That's great!" shouted the others.

Then Barbicane asked, "But what shape should it be?"

This last question started the others to argue again. Barbicane broke in. "My friends, I will decide that for you. But for now, let's stop arguing." The three men seemed puzzled, but they agreed.

"What metal shall we use for our cannon?" asked Maston.

"We must decide now," said Barbicane.

Each man ate several sandwiches and washed them down with a large cup of tea. Then they immediately went back to talking business.

"We must use a huge amount of metal, so we don't have much to choose from," Barbicane began.

"We should use alloy," said the general. "It's part copper, tin and brass."

"Good idea," answered Barbicane, "but it would be too expensive. I think cast iron would work better because it is cheap and easy to work with. Don't you agree, Major?"

"Yes," he answered.

"I am now going to ask our secretary to figure for us. We must know the weight of a cast iron cannon with a length of 900 feet. The walls will be six feet thick."

Maston wrote several numbers on a piece of paper. "The cannon will weigh 68,040 tons!"

"Cast iron is not expensive," said Barbicane. "It costs only two cents a pound. Maston, how much will the cast iron cost us?"

Once again, Maston worked out the numbers. "It will cost $2,721,600.00," he said.

With worried looks on their faces, the three men looked at Barbicane with wide eyes.

"Don't worry, my friends," Barbicane said. "We will have plenty of money."

The meeting ended. They met again the next night. The question of powder still had to be decided.

"What kind of powder should we use to launch our rocket?" asked the general.

"We'll use coarse powder. It burns faster than fine powder," said the major. They discussed it for a while. Then they all agreed. "How much powder should we use?" asked Barbicane.

"Two hundred thousand pounds," answered the general.

"Five hundred thousand is more like it!" yelled the major.

"Gentlemen," said Barbicane, "our cannon will be well built. It will be very strong. I am going to surprise Mr. Maston. I say we *double* his powder!"

"One million six hundred thousand pounds?" asked Maston, not believing his ears. He jumped out of his chair! "But then the cannon will have to be a half-mile long!"

"Yes," answered the major, smiling.

"I *demand* that much powder!" said Barbicane. "But it will be a different powder. We must use *guncotton* powder. It is made by soaking cotton in acid. It is the best powder for what we have planned. But it's *very* expensive."

"What does *that* matter?" said Maston, as the meeting ended.

Most people seemed to support the plan. But there was one person in the country who was against it. His name was Captain Nicholl. He was a scientist too. He held a grudge against Barbicane.

During the Civil War, Nicholl built armor. Barbicane built things that would go *through* armor. These men were opposites. They were rivals.

Nicholl wrote letters to the newspapers asking them not to support Barbicane's plan. He wrote against his money plans. He said that the plan was unsafe; that people living nearby would be hurt when the cannon was fired. Nicholl demanded the government stop the plan.

In the newspaper, THE RICHMOND ENQUIRER, Nicholl made a bet:

1. The Gun Club would not get enough money for the plan.
2. The 900-foot cannon could not be built.
3. The cannon could not be loaded correctly.
4. The cannon would burst when first lighted.
5. The cannon would shoot less than 6 miles, then it would fall back to earth.

Captain Nicholl bet a total of $15,000.00!

On October 19, he received an envelope. Inside, it said the following:

Baltimore, October 18
Bet Accepted.
Barbicane

The Bet

COMPREHENSION CHECK

Choose the best answer.

1. The cannon could be built as large as needed because
   _____a. a machine would be used to move it.
   _____b. a group of strong men would be used to move it.
   _____c. it would be made of a light-weight material.
   _____d. it would be built in the area where it was to launch the rocket.

2. It was decided that the length of the cannon would be
   _____a. 10,000 feet long.
   _____b. 5,000 feet long.
   _____c. 900 feet long.
   _____d. 9 feet long.

3. Barbicane told the committee that
   _____a. *he* would decide what shape the cannon would be.
   _____b. Maston would choose the shape of the cannon.
   _____c. the General would choose the shape of the cannon.
   _____d. they would all decide on the shape of the cannon.

4. During the meeting, the men
   _____a. became very tired.
   _____b. ate sandwiches and drank tea.
   _____c. became drunk.
   _____d. became disappointed in the plan.

5. The General's idea was to use a metal alloy for the cannon's material, but it was too
   _____a. light.
   _____b. heavy.
   _____c. cheap.
   _____d. expensive.

6. It was decided that the cannon would be made of
   _____a. a heavy wood.
   _____b. a cheap metal.
   _____c. tin.
   _____d. cast iron.

7. The length of the cannon would be
   _____a. four times the rocket's length.
   _____b. three times the rocket's length.
   _____c. thirty times the rocket's length.
   _____d. forty times the rocket's length.

8. Captain Nicholl and Impey Barbicane
   _____a. disagreed about most things.
   _____b. supported each other's ideas.
   _____c. were old boyhood friends.
   _____d. were good neighbors.

9. Another name for this story could be
   _____a. "An Unsafe Plan."
   _____b. "Unfriendly Rivals."
   _____c. "A Hungry Committee."
   _____d. "A Worried Committee."

10. This story is mainly about
    _____a. Impey Barbicane's plan to raise money.
    _____b. why Captain Nicholl dislikes Barbicane.
    _____c. men who argue about how to build a cannon.
    _____d. men who work together to make an idea happen.

Check your answers with the key on page 67.

This page may be reproduced for classroom use.

The Bet

VOCABULARY CHECK

bet	demand	expensive	immediately	length	powder

I. Sentences to Finish

Fill in the blank in each sentence with the correct key word from the box above.

1. I made a _____ with Tom that I would win the race.

2. The shoes were too _____ , so I didn't buy them.

3. The stone became a fine _____ when I hit it with the hammer.

4. When Maria's new toy broke, Mother went to the store to _____ her money back.

5. When I go to bed at night, I _____ fall asleep.

6. The _____ of the room is twelve feet.

II. Matching

Write the letter of the correct meaning from Column B next to the key word in Column A

Column A	Column B
_____1. length	a. the promise to give money or some other thing to another if he is right and you are wrong
_____2. powder	b. to ask for as a right, or with authority
_____3. bet	c. a substance that's reduced to dust
_____4. demand	d. without delay; at once
_____5. immediately	e. having a high price; costing much
_____6. expensive	f. the measure of how long a thing is

Check your answers with the key on page 70.

This page may be reproduced for classroom use.

Off to Florida

PREPARATION

Key Words

alligator (al´ə gāt´ər) a large reptile with a long body and tail that lives in rivers in the Southeastern U.S.
> *Paula thought the <u>alligator</u> in the river was a floating stick.*

arrangement (ə rānj´ment) plan; preparation
> *The families made an <u>arrangement</u> to meet for dinner next week.*

climate (klī´mət) the usual weather conditions of a place over a long period of time
> *Michigan's <u>climate</u> is made up of the four seasons.*

degree (di grē´) 1. a unit that is used in measuring angles and parts of circles. It is shown by the symbol, °.
> *There are 360 <u>degrees</u> in a circle.*

2. a unit for measuring temperature
> *When the temperature reached 90 <u>degrees</u>, I felt awfully hot.*

tropical (trop´ə kl) having to do with the tropics which are two imaginary circles around the earth, parallel to the equator. The tropics often means the area between these two circles.
> *The hot breeze made Amy feel like she was on a <u>tropical</u> island.*

zero (zir´ ō) 1. a point marked as 0 on the scale of a thermometer or some other scale
> *Last winter it was below <u>zero</u> for four days in a row!*

2. none; nothing
> *Our team had <u>zero</u> wins last year.*

Off to Florida

Necessary Words

latitude   (lat´ə tüd)   distance north or south from the equator that is measured in degrees
> *The <u>latitude</u> 40 degrees north goes through the United States.*

malaria   (mə lãr´ē ə)   a disease in which a person keeps having chills and fever. It is caused by mosquitoes.
> *Ann's Uncle Peter caught <u>Malaria</u> while living in Africa.*

project   (proj´ekt)   a plan
> *We must complete our <u>project</u> by Friday.*

People

Seminole   a member of any of the North American Indian peoples who settled in Florida

Places

New Orleans   a city in the state of Louisiana
Tampa   a city in the state of Florida
Union   The United States of America

Off to Florida

Barbicane and his party explore Florida on horseback.

Preview: 1. Read the name of the story.
               2. Look at the picture.
               3. Read the sentence under the picture.
               4. Read the first paragraph of the story.
               5. Then answer the following question.

You learned from your preview that the launch had to take place in an area with

___a. a good climate.
___b. a wet climate.
___c. a cold climate.
___d. a windy climate.

Turn to the Comprehension Check on page 34 for the right answer.

Now read the story.

Read to find out how long it took to build the cannon.

Off to Florida

It was important to find the right place for the experiment. The cannon would have to be fired from a special place; a place between zero and twenty-eight degrees of latitude. This place must have a good climate. Exactly where would the cannon be made?

Early in October, the gun Club held another meeting. J.T. Maston spoke first. "I demand we talk about where we will shoot our cannon from?" he said. "I think it is important that the cannon be launched from the United States."

"Of course," said many of the members in agreement.

"Then it's decided? We must go to war with Mexico. It is the only country with a twenty-eighth parallel. Now we have a reason for war!" spoke Maston.

"No, no," cried the members of the committee.

"But we must!" said Maston, angrily.

"Maston, you may no longer speak!" yelled Barbicane. "There is no need for war! The twenty-eighth parallel, my dear Maston, also runs across Florida and Texas. And these states have the right latitudes we need."

Shortly after this talk, men from both Texas and Florida came to Baltimore. They fought all the time. They both wanted the honor of shooting the cannon from their land. Florida said Texas had the disease malaria. Then Texas said that Florida had many fevers, too. Florida claimed to be more American; that it had belonged to the Union longer than Texas had. Everyone thought the two groups would fight a bloody battle in the streets! Barbicane was going crazy; the fighting had to stop. He called another meeting.

"Texas has many large towns," spoke Barbicane. "They all fight each other for the honor of shooting our cannon. But Florida has only one large town. Our choice is clear. Florida it is!" he said.

One important choice had been made. But there was another problem to worry about. They needed money. Millions of dollars! This was an American project. But they needed more than American money. Barbicane asked the world for help. Many countries gave thousands of dollars. But Spain could only give $11.00. And England gave zero money! The Gun Club received over five million dollars! All this money would be needed to make the cannon. It would also help feed and house the people working on the project.

On October 20, an important contract was signed. It was with the Cold Spring Company. The contract said that this company would be in charge of making the cannon. They would make arrangements to hire all the workers. The work was to be done by October 15th of the next year. The cannon would be made in Tampa, Florida.

Everyone wanted to learn more about Tampa. Barbicane made the arrangements and left for Florida. He went with J.T. Maston and the major. Mr. Murchison, manager of the Cold Spring Company, went also. They traveled by ship.

As they got closer to Florida, Barbicane noticed something. He saw that the land was flat. It had few plants or trees. The men stepped off the ship.

"Tomorrow we will explore this land on horseback!" said Barbicane.

The next morning, they found 50 horses under their hotel window! With a man on every horse! Each man carried a rifle.

"We carry rifles because of the Seminoles, sir," explained a young man.

"Rifles?" asked Barbicane.

"It's for your safety, sir," the young man said.

"Thank you," Barbicane answered.

They left at 5 o'clock in the morning. It was a tropical 84 degrees. The climate was hot and sticky. By ten o'clock in the morning, the group had traveled 12 miles. The trees looked very tropical. They had long vines and grew fruit. As they rode, they saw many creeks and streams. Many were filled with alligators which grew as long as eighteen feet. Everyone feared the alligators.

Finally, all the wet country was gone. The trees became smaller and the land was flatter.

"At last!" said Barbicane. "Here are the pine trees!"

"And Indians!" add the major.

A few Seminoles stood in the distance. They held long spears and fired rifles into the air. Barbicane and his party were not afraid. They rode for a while longer.

"Stop!" said Barbicane. "Does this place have a name?"

"It's called Stone Hill," answered one of the men.

Barbicane got off his horse. He took out his measuring tools. A short time later, Barbicane was done.

"We will build our cannon here!" he spoke.

That night, Barbicane and his men returned to Tampa. Murchison left for New Orleans. There he hired workers for the project. Eight days later he returned. He brought fifteen hundred workers. There were mechanics, smiths, and miners. Many of them brought their families with them. On October 31, at ten o'clock in the morning, they were in Tampa.

It took eight months to prepare for the casting. On July 8th it was done. The casting was set for the next day. A party was planned.

"The casting cannot be make public!" Barbicane said. He knew there would be sparks and great heat. He was afraid it would be too dangerous for people to be near. Only Gun Club members could watch the casting of the cannon.

At noon the next day it happened. The ground shook! Clouds of smoke flew high into the air. It was done.

Off to Florida

COMPREHENSION CHECK

Choose the best answer.

1. Maston felt it necessary to go to war with
   _____a. Moscow.
   _____b. Mongolia.
   _____c. Morocco.
   _____d. Mexico.

2. Maston thought Mexico was the only country with
   _____a. enough land for the project.
   _____b. enough people to help with the project.
   _____c. right angles.
   _____d. a twenty-eighth parallel.

3. Maston wanted to make Mexico
   _____a. part of the United States.
   _____b. a poor country.
   _____c. a rich country.
   _____d. part of the project.

4. Barbicane
   _____a. thought Maston's idea of war was a good one.
   _____b. was angry with Maston's talk of war.
   _____c. laughed at Maston's talk of war.
   _____d. made plans to go to war with Mexico immediately.

5. Barbicane told Maston that the twenty-eighth parallel also ran through
   _____a. Florida and Hawaii.
   _____b. Florida and California.
   _____c. Florida and Texas.
   _____d. Florida and Georgia.

6. Millions of dollars were needed for the project. Why did Barbicane ask the *world* for help?
   _____a. They needed more than American money.
   _____b. America had no money.
   _____c. Other countries had plenty of money to give.
   _____d. He wanted the whole world to be a part of the project.

7. What was the name of the company that would make the cannon?
   _____a. The Cold Spring Company
   _____b. The Gold Spring Company
   _____c. The Cast Iron Company
   _____d. The Cannon Makers

8. What was the name of the spot where the cannon would be built?
   _____a. Cannon Hill
   _____b. Stone Hill
   _____c. Seminole Hill
   _____d. Tampa Hill

9. Another name for this story could be
   _____a. "Maston Wants War!"
   _____b. "Exploring Florida."
   _____c. "A Cannon is Cast."
   _____d. "The Stone Hill Gang."

10. This story is mainly about
    _____a. how the committee went about choosing the right spot for the launch.
    _____b. taking a trip to the tropics.
    _____c. the Seminole Indians who lived in Florida.
    _____d. how long it takes to build a cannon.

Check your answers with the key on page 67.

Off to Florida

VOCABULARY CHECK

alligator	arrangement	climate	degree	tropical	zero

I. Sentences to Finish

Fill in the blank in each sentence with the correct key word from the box above.

1. Tom and I made an _____ to meet for dinner at six o'clock.

2. The hot sun raised the pool's temperature one _____ .

3. Hawaii is a _____ island in the Pacific.

4 In certain parts of the country, _____ meat is eaten quite often.

5. I just love the cold weather, but my wife enjoys a warmer _____ .

6. At 32 degrees below _____, water turns to ice.

II. Word Search

All the words from the box above are hidden in the puzzle below. They may be written from left to right, or up and down. As you find each word, put a circle around it. One word, that is not a key word, has been done for you.

```
U  A  W  E  L  E  T  R  O
T  R  O  P  I  C  A  L  D
R  R  C  X  S  L  L  Z  E
O  A  L  C  E  I  L  E  G
P  N  I  O  M  M  I  R  R
A  G  M  L  P  A  G  A  X
R  E  A  D  P  T  A  L  G
R  M  A  F  N  E  T  L  G
A  E  L  Z  E  R  O  Q  R
N  N  L  D  E  G  R  E  E
G  T  Z  E  R  T  R  O  D
```

Check your answers with the key on page 70.

This page may be reproduced for classroom use.

A Message to Barbicane

PREPARATION

Key Words

accept (ak sept´) to take what is offered or given
Paul did not <u>accept</u> the candy the man held out.

date (dāt) a period of time; a special place in time
Theresa's <u>date</u> of birth is March 4th.

December (di sem´bər) the last month of the year
<u>December</u> is always a busy month because of the holidays.

disgrace (dis grās´) loss of respect or honor; shame
It was a <u>disgrace</u> that Mike cheated on his math test.

examination (eg zam´ə nā´shən) the act or process of looking something over carefully
The cowboy gave a careful <u>examination</u> of the horse before buying it.

impatient (im pā´shənt) not patient; not willing to put up with something such as a delay or pain
The crowd grew <u>impatient</u> waiting for the store to open.

A Message to Barbicane

Necessary Words

cablegram   (kā´bl gram)   a thick, heavy, strong line made of strands of wire twisted together that carries messages under the ocean
> *Tim was excited when he received a <u>cablegram</u> from Uncle Todd.*

comment   (kom´ent)   a note or remark that explains or gives an opinion
> *The teacher's <u>comment</u> about my test made me feel good.*

congratulated   (kən grach´ə lāt əd)   to have expressed happiness to another person because of that person's success or good luck.
> *Tony's parents <u>congratulated</u> him for winning the race.*

platform   (plat´fôrm)   a flat surface or stage higher than the ground or floor around it
> *As the men worked on the billboard, their <u>platform</u> needed to go higher.*

toast   (tōst)   the act of honoring a person or thing by holding up one's glass, saying some words, and drinking
> *"Let's make a <u>toast</u> to Betty to wish her well in her new home."*

volcano   (vol kā´nō)   an opening in the earth's surface that forms when melted rock from deep inside the earth is thrown up
> *The people rebuilt their village away from the <u>volcano</u>.*

People

Michel Ardan   is a 42 year old Frenchman who wants to be shot to the moon in the Gun Club's cannon.

Places

France   is a country in western Europe.

A Message to Barbicane

The Gun Club members grow impatient waiting to go near the cannon.

Preview: 1. Read the name of the story.
                   2. Look at the picture.
                   3. Read the sentence under the picture.
                   4. Read the first two paragraphs of the story.
                   5. Then answer the following question.

You learned from your preview that

___a. no one wanted to go near the cannon.

___b. no one had interest in the project anymore.

___c. the Gun Club members were excited and impatient to take a closer look.

___d. the Gun Club members were unhappy with the cannon's size and shape.

Turn to the Comprehension Check on page 40 for the right answer.

Now read the story.

Read to find out about the letter Barbicane receives.

A Message to Barbicane

The cannon that would send a rocket to the moon had been made. Barbicane and his friends watched from a nearby hill. Huge clouds of smoke rose into the sky. An Indian passing by might have thought a new volcano was forming. Two weeks after the cannon was cast, smoke still hung in the sky. It was hard to accept that these clouds were not made by a tornado or a storm; that they were made by man.

The Gun Club members were impatient! They wanted to go near the cannon. But the ground was still too hot to stand on.

"The date is August 10!" said J.T. Maston one day. "It is less than four months until December. We can't even go near the cannon! We won't be ready on time!"

But by August 22, Barbicane and the other Gun Club members were able to stand at the top of Stone Hill.

"At last!" sighed Barbicane.

For the next month, men worked on the cannon. Finally, on September 22, it was checked. Special tools were used to check it and make sure it would work right. It was cooled and ready for action!

J.T. Maston was excited. He leaned far into the cannon. He almost fell into the nine-hundred foot tube! Colonel Bloomsberry saved him.

"Thank you!" he said to the colonel.

The cannon work area had been open to the public since September 23. It was under examination all the time. People from all over the country came to visit Tampa. Some people moved there too. New houses were everywhere. Churches and schools were being built too. Businesses were opened overnight. The city was growing fast.

Some of the people from Tampa were unhappy that they had not been allowed to watch the casting of the cannon. This was for their own safety, but they wouldn't accept this as a reason. Some said that it was a disgrace not to be allowed down *into* the cannon. They wouldn't accept "no" for an answer! So Barbicane agreed. But he decided to make it worth the bother. He charged the people money for examination of the cannon. It cost $5.00 for each man, woman, or child. Each person stood on a platform that took them down into the huge cannon.

But the public was not the first to go down into the cannon. The first to go down were members of the Gun Club. Who else?

On September 25, a cage lowered Barbicane, Maston, and many other important members. They went down, down, down!

"It is hot down here," said the major.

And what excitement there was! Down inside the cannon a table was set for all of them. The best wines were served, and wonderful food came down from above. It was noisy. They all congratulated each other. Toasts were given by many. They drank to the moon, the earth, and the Gun Club. A huge crowd of people gathered above. They joined in the party. There were cheers and shouts of joy. J.T. Maston was quite excited. He would not have traded places with anyone that day. Not even if today was the date in December when they would fire the cannon!

But soon the Gun Club members became impatient again. Now they had to wait two more months until the cannon could shoot its rocket to the moon. All at once they had nothing to help them pass the time.

On September 30, at 3:47 P.M., a message was delivered to Barbicane. It came by cablegram.

He opened the envelope and read the message. His hands shook with excitement. His lips turned pale. This is what was written:
PARIS, FRANCE
SEPTEMBER 30, 4:00 A.M.
BARBICANE
TAMPA, FLORIDA, U.S.A.
REPLACE THE CANNON SHELL YOU HAVE. PUT IN A LIGHTER SHELL, INSTEAD. *I* WILL GO TO THE MOON IN IT. I WILL COME ON THE SHIP NAMED ATLANTIC.

MICHEL ARDAN

Was it a joke? Was it all made up by someone? Before Barbicane could think, people learned about the cablegram. Everyone was talking. The news of Michel Ardan's idea was spreading across the country fast!

Barbicane called together his Gun Club friends. He quietly read the message aloud to them.

"A disgrace!"

"Someone has lost his mind!"

"It must be a joke!"

The members couldn't believe it. For some time, people made comments like these. They laughed at the idea. Only J.T. Maston was excited about it. "Now *that's* an idea!" he said.

"Yes," said Major Elphiston. "It's all right to have an idea like that. As long as you don't plan on really *doing* it!"

"Why *shouldn't* he do it?" Maston asked.

The people in Tampa were talking, but not about Michel Ardan. They were talking about J.T. Maston. They couldn't believe he thought Michel Ardan would really do it! How could a man ever think he could be shot to the moon from a cannon!

A Message to Barbicane

COMPREHENSION CHECK

Choose the best answer.

1. After the cannon was cast, why wouldn't anyone go near it?
_____a. The ground around the cannon was too cold to stand on.
_____b. The ground around the cannon was too hot to stand on.
_____c. They were afraid.
_____d. They couldn't see it through all the smoke.

2. The cannon was cast early in
_____a. December.
_____b. October.
_____c. August.
_____d. April.

3. The cannon was finished and ready for action in
_____a. September.
_____b. October.
_____c. November.
_____d. December.

4. The cannon's tube was
_____a. 10-feet long.
_____b. 15-feet long.
_____c. 90- feet long.
_____d. 900-feet long.

5. Who saved J.T. Maston from falling down into the cannon's tube?
_____a. Impey Barbicane
_____b. Colonel Bloomsberry
_____c. Major Elphiston
_____d. Michel Ardan

6. As word of the project spread around the world, the city of Tampa
_____a. became a poor city.
_____b. became a rich city.
_____c. became a dirty city.
_____d. grew.

7. When Barbicane and other members of the Gun Club wnet down into the cannon, what did they find there?
_____a. A table set for all of them
_____b. A huge crowd
_____c. A wine-tasting party
_____d. Two men fighting

8. Michel Ardan sent a cablegram to Barbicane that said
_____a. he wanted to join the Gun Club.
_____b. he did not approve of the project.
_____c. he wanted to be shot from the cannon to the moon.
_____d. he wanted to go to the moon in a ship named *Atlantic*.

9. Another name for this story could be
_____a. "A Ship Named Atlantic."
_____b. "Michel's Joke."
_____c. "Michel Ardan's Idea."
_____d. "The Surprise Party."

10. This story is mainly about
_____a. men working together to complete a project.
_____b. a crazy man who wants to go to the moon.
_____c. how the city of Tampa grew.
_____d. the Gun Club's surprise party.

Check your answers with the key on page 67.

This page may be reproduced for classroom use.

A Message to Barbicane

VOCABULARY CHECK

accept	date	December	disgrace	examination	impatient

I. Sentences to Finish

Fill in the blank in each sentence with the correct key word from the box above.

1. Sometimes Greg becomes _____ with his little brother.

2. _____ is the last month of the year.

3. The thief brought _____ to his family.

4. Children should never _____ candy from a stranger.

5. The doctor gave a careful _____ of my throat.

6. The _____ of the trial is set for December 5th.

II. Mixed-up Words

First, unscramble the letters in Column A to spell out the key words. Then, match the key words with the right meaning in Column B by drawing a line from the words to the meaning.

Column A

1. pimattien _____

2. cragside _____

3. tapecc _____

4. tead _____

5. noxinetaami _____

6. Dreebmec _____

Column B

a. the last month of the year

b. not willing to put up with delay or pain

c. loss of respect or honor; shame

d. to take what is offered or given

e. a period of time; a special place in time

f. the act or process of looking something over carefully

Check your answers with the key on page 70.

This page may be reproduced for classroom use.

Michel Ardan Arrives

PREPARATION

Key Words

accent (ak´sent) the different way of saying words and phrases by people from a certain area or country
> *The man from Texas spoke with a southern <u>accent</u>.*

artist (är´tist) a person who is skilled in painting, sculpture, music, or any other area of art
> *A young <u>artist</u> in our town painted flowers on the sidewalks.*

champion (cham´pē ∂n) a person who is judged to be best in a contest or sport
> *My brother Chad was the state <u>champion</u> in wrestling.*

crazy (krā´zē) very foolish or unwise
> *I told Sally she was <u>crazy</u> when she said homework was fun!*

flight (flīt) the act or way of flying or moving through space
> *Paul couldn't wait to go on his first airplane <u>flight</u>.*

news (nüz) something told as having just happened
> *Tammy told us the exciting <u>news</u> that she was going to be an aunt.*

Michel Ardan Arrives

Necessary Words

anchor	(ang´kər)	a heavy object that is let down into the water by a chain to keep a ship or boat in place *The huge ship let its <u>anchor</u> drop when it reached port.*
cell	(sel)	a small, plain room in a prison or jail *The policeman threw the robber in a jail <u>cell</u>.*
intelligent	(in tel´ə jənt)	being able to learn, think, and understand well *Pat made the <u>intelligent</u> choice not to smoke.*
port	(pôrt)	a place where boats and ships can dock safely; harbor *The <u>port</u> in the city of New Orleans is one of the busiest in the world.*
risk	(risk)	the chance of losing, failing, or getting hurt; danger *Beth took a <u>risk</u> by riding her skateboard in the street.*

Michel Ardan Arrives

A large crowd waits eagerly for Michel Ardan's arrival.

Preview: 1. Read the name of the story.
2. Look at the picture.
3. Read the sentence under the picture.
4. Read the first two paragraphs of the story.
5. Then answer the following question.

You learned from your preview that
___a. most people had never heard of Michel Ardan.
___b. people around the world had heard of Michel Ardan.
___c. Michel Ardan was a crazy man.
___d. Michel Ardan was always telling jokes.

Turn to the Comprehension Check on page 46 for the right answer.

Now read the story.

Read to find out what Michel Ardan has to say about his idea.

Michel Ardan Arrives

Barbicane, surprised that anyone wanted to go to the moon, could think of nothing but Ardan's message. *"He wants to go to the moon in our cannon?"* Barbicane thought the man must be crazy. He thought the man should be locked away in a cell.

The news of Michel Ardan's offer to be shot to the moon was becoming more well known every day. People from all over the world had heard about it. And most were still joking about it.

But some people were taking Mr. Ardan seriously. "Why shouldn't a man make a flight to the moon?" some of them asked themselves.

A great number of people could not be sure if this man was real. Had someone sent the cable as a joke?

Soon a crowd of people gathered outside of Barbicane's house. They thought he could answer some of their questions. When Barbicane appeared, the crowd fell silent. Except for one man. "Is the man called Michel Ardan really coming? Is he coming from France to America?"

"Gentlemen," Barbicane replied, "I do not know any more about it than you do."

"Surely this man is mad!" a young man in the crowd shouted.

"The man must be crazy!" shouted another.

"Time will tell," answered Barbicane. "But for now, let *us* send a message."

Barbicane walked to the telegraph office. A crowd of people followed him. There, he sent a message to France. He asked the following questions:

IS THERE A SHIP NAMED ATLANTA? DID IT JUST LEAVE EUROPE? DOES IT HAVE A PASSENGER ABOARD NAMED MICHEL ARDAN?

Two hours later Barbicane got the news. The answer was as follows:

THE SHIP ATLANTA SAILED YESTERDAY. IT IS HEADED FOR TAMPA.

A FRENCHMAN AND ARTIST NAMED MICHEL ARDAN IS ON BOARD.

Barbicane read this message to the crowd.

"He *must* be mad," Barbicane thought to himself. "He'll never make the flight!"

On October 20, everything seemed to stop. Businesses closed up shop. Schools closed their doors. Ships stayed at port. Nobody wanted to risk missing the arrival of the *Atlanta*.

That evening, at 6 o'clock, the *Atlanta* dropped anchor in Tampa Bay. The crowd of people stood silent. They had waited all day to get a look at Michel Ardan. Barbicane was the first to step aboard.

"Michel Ardan!" he shouted.

"Here," a voice replied.

Here is what Barbicane saw. Michel Ardan was about 42 years old. Tall, and a little round shouldered. His hair was bushy like that of a lion's. He had a mustache that looked like a cat's whiskers. His eyes were like a cat's too. He was intelligent-looking, with strong, powerful arms. He wore a big white shirt with long, puffy sleeves. It was open at the collar. Who had ever seen a man like this one? He was an artist by trade, but he looked more like a fine champion.

The crowd cheered with delight because Michel Ardan was here! When the crowd grew large around him, Ardan went to his cabin on the ship. Barbicane followed him.

"Are you Impey Barbicane?" asked Ardan.

"Yes I am," he answered. "Was your cable some sort of joke?" he continued. "Do you think you can *really* do it?"

"Of course!" Ardan answered.

"Will anything make you change your mind?" Barbicane asked, hoping that he would.

"Nothing can!" Ardan answered.

"Have you thought it over carefully?" came another question from Barbicane.

"I can't waste time thinking it over! I have a chance to do what no man has done before. And I'm going to do it!" said Ardan.

"But do you have a *plan*?" asked Barbicane.

Gather your friends. Gather the city, the state, the whole country! I will tell my story one time to all!"

And that is what Barbicane did. He told the people what Ardan had said and they became excited. J.T. Maston was the most excited of all. "Ardan's a champion!" he shouted.

The next day a huge tent was set up outside of town. Three thousand people stood in the heat waiting to hear what Ardan had to say. At three o'clock in the afternoon it was time. The Gun Club members stood near Ardan. The crowd cheered for him. He was their champion. Then the crowd became silent, listening carefully for Ardan's words; his French accent was at times hard to understand.

"Someday the oceans will be crossed in one short day," he began. "And Man will someday travel to the moon. Many people don't believe it, but I believe it is true. And I will be the first! My flight will take only ninety-seven hours. I believe that within twenty years half the people of earth will have visited the moon!"

"Three cheers for Michel Ardan!" the crowd roared.

"Does anyone have any questions?" Ardan asked the crowd with his accent.

"Do you think there could be life on the moon?" came a voice from the crowd.

"I am not a scientist, I am only an artist. So I do not know for sure. But I believe that there *could* be life there!" said Ardan, as he looked up at the sky.

The crowd cheered once again. They yelled in support of the Frenchman. He was their hero.

Michel Ardan Arrives

COMPREHENSION CHECK

Choose the best answer.

1. Most people
   _____a. laughed at Michel Ardan's idea.
   _____b. thought that Michel Ardan was lying.
   _____c. believed that Michel's idea was possible.
   _____d. warned Michel Ardan not to do it.

2. Barbicane sent a message to France
   _____a. to pass the time.
   _____b. to please the crowd.
   _____c. to tell Michel Ardan no to come.
   _____d. to satisfy himself and the crowd that the cable he received was not a joke.

3. When Barbicane received the news that Ardan was on the *Atlanta* and sailing for Tampa, he was
   _____a. pleased.
   _____b. surprised.
   _____c. worried.
   _____d. happy.

4. The *Atlanta* dropped anchor
   _____a. in the morning.
   _____b. in the afternoon.
   _____c. in the early evening.
   _____d. in the middle of the night.

5. Michel Ardan
   _____a. was a butcher.
   _____b. was a fisherman.
   _____c. was an artist.
   _____d. was a peddler.

6. Barbicane was hoping that Michel Ardan would
   _____a. change his mind and forget about his crazy idea.
   _____b. go back to France.
   _____c. take a long vacation.
   _____d. disappear.

7. Michel Ardan told his story to a crowd of about
   _____a. ten thousand people.
   _____b. three thousand people.
   _____c. three million people.
   _____d. three hundred people.

8. Michel Ardan believed that one day it would be common for Man to
   _____a. travel through space.
   _____b. travel the world.
   _____c. see into the future.
   _____d. sail the seas.

9. Another name for this story could be
   _____a. "The Life of an Artist."
   _____b. "A Hero Comes to Tampa."
   _____c. "A Ship Sails to Florida."
   _____d. "Mr. Ardan's Flight to the Moon."

10. This story is mainly about
    _____a. a man who was not afraid to risk his life for a chance to do something different.
    _____b. a man who proved everyone wrong.
    _____c. a man looking for adventure.
    _____d. Michel Ardan's visit to America.

Check your answers with the key on page 67.

This page may be reproduced for classroom use.

Michel Ardan Arrives

VOCABULARY CHECK

accent	artist	champion	crazy	flight	news

I. Sentences to Finish

Fill in the blank in each sentence with the correct key word from the box above.

1. The _____ of the race, Dominick Vaz, received a blue ribbon.

2. The airplane _____ to New York took five hours.

3. We listened carefully to the speaker because he spoke with an _____ .

4. Bradley likes to draw. He hopes to become an _____ someday.

5. The _____ about my best friend moving made me sad.

6. He must be _____ to think he can fool his mother.

II. Using the Words

On the lines below, write six of your own sentences using the key words from the box above. Use each word once, drawing a line under the key word.

1. _____

2. _____

3. _____

4. _____

5. _____

6. _____

Check your answers with the key on page 71.

This page may be reproduced for classroom use.

The Quarrel

PREPARATION

Key Words

fact	(fakt)	something that can be proved *I can't deny the <u>fact</u> that I was late.*
gentleman	(jen´tl mən)	a man who is polite and kind *The <u>gentleman</u> opened the store door for the shoppers.*
honesty	(on´is tē)	the condition of being truthful *In all <u>honesty</u>, I did forget to take out the garbage.*
hotel	(hō tel´)	a building where travelers can rent rooms, buy meals, hold meetings and such *Our vacation was fun because our <u>hotel</u> had an indoor swimming pool.*
mention	(men´shən)	to speak or write about in just a few words *Please <u>mention</u> when our homework is due.*
quarrel	(kwôr´əl)	an argument or disagreement *Ben had a loud <u>quarrel</u> with his brother Mike.*

The Quarrel

Necessary Words

challenged   (chal´əngd)   called to take part in a contest or fight; dared
The bully <u>challenged</u> Pete in the car race.

duel   (dü´əl)   a formal fight between two people armed with weapons
They fought the <u>duel</u> with swords.

enemy   (en´ə mē)   a person, group or country that hates another or fights against another
In World War II, Germany was the <u>enemy</u> of the United States.

platform   (plat´fôrm)   a flat surface or stage higher than the ground or floor around it
The rock band played their music from a huge <u>platform</u> stage.

The Quarrel

"I suppose you think you are brave," spoke a stranger in the crowd to Michel Ardan.

Preview: 1. Read the name of the story.
                   2. Look at the picture.
                   3. Read the sentence under the picture.
                   4. Read the first four paragraphs of the story.
                   5. Then answer the following question.

You learned from your preview that the stranger in the crowd told Ardan that

___a. there was no air on the moon.
___b. there was no water on the moon.
___c. there was no food on the moon.
___d. there really wasn't any moon at all.

Turn to the Comprehension Check on page 52 for the right answer.

Now read the story.

Read to find out who Ardan gets a letter from.

The Quarrel

Michel Ardan, the Frenchman, spoke to a large crowd about his plans to be shot to the moon from a cannon.

"What do *you* know about the moon?" a gentleman asked loudly.

All eyes turned to the stranger who had spoken. He was tall and thin, with a thick beard.

"You say there is life on the moon. Maybe...but it is a fact that there is no *air* on the moon," the stranger said.

"Who says there is no air on the moon?" Ardan demanded.

"Scientists!" answered the stranger.

"Let me just say," said Ardan, "that scientists have been wrong before!"

His voice, becoming louder, the stranger answered, "I suppose you think you are brave!"

"In all honesty," replied Ardan, "a man is only brave when he doesn't know about danger."

Barbicane had been watching the stranger closely.

"Do you know about the fact that volcanoes are on the moon?" asked the stranger.

"Only dead ones," Ardan answered.

"You will not be able to breathe!" the stranger shouted.

"Don't worry," replied Ardan. "I'll only breathe when I have to!"

The crowd cheered with delight. He was their hero.

"You will be smashed if you reach the moon!" the stranger continued.

Ardan remained calm. "My friend Barbicane will make something to protect me, so I am not worried."

"What about food and water?" asked the man.

"I will take enough to last one year," Ardan laughed.

"And how do you expect to return to the earth?" the stranger asked, his face becoming red with anger. He could not believe that Ardan was really going ahead with his plans.

"This is Man's first flight into space. I do not really expect to return to earth," Ardan answered.

The crowd fell silent.

The stranger spoke once more. "You are right, Ardan. You'll never return to earth. But you are not to blame!"

"Then who is?" came a voice from the crowd.

"*That gentleman!*" shouted the stranger, as he pointed to Barbicane.

Barbicane had been angered by this stranger all along, but now he wa really mad! He tried to grab the stranger, but he couldn't reach him. Hundreds of arms picked up the platform that Ardan and Barbicane shared and held it on their shoulders. They were carried with honor. But never once did the stranger's eyes leave Barbicane's.

Carried to Ardan's hotel, Ardan and Barbicane freed themselves from the crowd. Barbicane came face-to-face with the stranger. "Who are you?" Barbicane demanded.

"Captain Nicholl, the scientist!" he answered.

"My rival? It figures," said Barbicane.

"I challenge you to a duel," said Nicholl.

"Let's say, five o'clock in the morning," replied Barbicane.

"Good! We'll meet in the nearby woods. And bring your rifle," said Nicholl.

"But of course," answered Barbicane.

That night, as Michel lay sleeping, there came a pounding on his hotel door.

"Open your door!" cried a voice.

Ardan opened the door. J.T. Maston burst in. "Yesterday, Barbicane and another man had a quarrel. The man challenged Barbicane to a duel in the woods. We must stop them!" Maston exploded.

Ardan dressed quickly. He had to think of something fast to save Barbicane.

"Each man will hide in the woods with his rifle. They will hunt each other like animals!" Maston said with alarm.

Soon they reached the woods. They were surprised when they found Captain Nicholl. He was busy helping a hurt bird escape from a huge spider's web.

"Don't pretend to be a kind man," Ardan told him.

"What are *you* doing here?" Nicholl asked.

"In all honesty, we've come to keep you from killing Barbicane," answered Ardan.

"I've been looking for him for two hours! Where is he hiding?" asked the captain.

"He is here," said Ardan. "And we will find him."

"And I will kill him when you do!" said Nicholl.

"No you won't!" shouted Ardan. "You see, I have an offer to make to the two of you that will stop your quarrel."

"Really? And what would that be?"

"I will mention it when Barbicane is here," answered Ardan.

The three men walked through the woods and soon found Barbicane. He was sitting under a tree, writing.

"There he is!" Maston yelled.

Barbicane was surprised to see them. He had almost forgotten about the duel until he saw Nicholl.

"Captain, I'm ready now!" spoke Barbicane.

"Wait!" shouted Ardan. "If you can't agree with each other, agree with me. Why don't both of you come to the moon *with* me?"

Barbicane and Nicholl looked at each other, then at Ardan. They both agreed with the idea.

On October 18, they shot the cannon for practice. They wanted to see how well it would work. But before placing a man inside the shell, they would test animals first. A big cat and Maston's pet squirrel were placed inside the cannon shell.

"R-O-A-R!" The cannon was fired! It rose in the air to about one thousand feet, then fell into the water. Men quickly pulled it onto land.

It had only been five minutes since the animals had been placed in the shell. The shell was opened. The cat jumped out, but there was no sign of the squirrel. Had the cat eaten it?

No one ever found out what had become of the squirrel. But everyone was pleased that the landing went well.

And Michel Ardan was pleased when, two days later, he got an important message. It was from the President of the United States. Ardan had been make a citizen of the United States!

The Quarrel

Preview Answer:

a. there was no air on the moon.

COMPREHENSION CHECK

Choose the best answer.

1. Michel Ardan spoke to the crowd about
   _____a. life in France.
   _____b. how to become an artist.
   _____c. his plans to visit England.
   _____d. his plans to visit the moon.

2. The crowd
   _____a. was eager to hear what Ardan had to say.
   _____b. did not care what Ardan had to say.
   _____c. showed little interest in Michel Ardan.
   _____d. laughed at Ardan's ideas.

3. The stranger in the crowd
   _____a. was Ardan's brother.
   _____b. was the man who had bet Barbicane $15,000.00 that his plan would fail.
   _____c. knew nothing about space travel.
   _____d. was just a stranger who liked to argue.

4. Captain Nicholl was
   _____a. a member of the Gun Club.
   _____b. an artist.
   _____c. a scientist.
   _____d. a trouble maker.

5. Captain Nicholl challenged Barbicane to a duel with
   _____a. rifles.
   _____b. swords.
   _____c. knives.
   _____d. sticks.

6. Ardan stopped the duel when he asked Barbicane and Nicholl
   _____a. to go home.
   _____b. to forgive each other.
   _____c. to join him on his trip to the moon.
   _____d. share their ideas.

7. What was placed inside the cannon shell on its first practice shot?
   _____a. A cat and a squirrel
   _____b. A cat and a dog
   _____c. A bird and a cat
   _____d. A squirrel and a frog

8. The President of the United States sent Ardan a message telling him that
   _____a. he was a hero.
   _____b. he had been made a citizen of the United States.
   _____c. he was not to carry on with his plan.
   _____d. he was to return to France right away.

9. Another name for this story could be
   _____a. "The Cat that Ate the Squirrel."
   _____b. "Barbicane's Honor."
   _____c. "Challenged to a Duel."
   _____d. "Captain Nicholl Saves a Bird."

10. This story is mainly about
    _____a. how two enemies became good friends.
    _____b. a duel in the woods.
    _____c. a cat who ate a squirrel.
    _____d. how Ardan's quick thinking helped save Barbicane.

Check your answers with the key on page 67.

This page may be reproduced for classroom use.

The Quarrel

VOCABULARY CHECK

fact	gentleman	honesty	hotel	mention	quarrel

I. Sentences to Finish
Fill in the blank in each sentence with the correct key word from the box above.

1. It is a _____ that dogs chase cats.

2. I thought I would _____ that today is my birthday.

3. Linda and Kathy have not spoken since their _____ .

4. The _____ where I stayed has a lovely view of the beach.

5. He answered my questions with _____ .

6. The _____ helped the woman carry her bags.

II. True or False
Are the statements true or false? Check one line.

	TRUE	FALSE
1. If someone <u>mentions</u> something to you, you are being spoken to.	_____	_____
2. If you <u>quarrel</u> with someone, you are getting along.	_____	_____
3. A <u>hotel</u> is a place where sick people go to get well.	_____	_____
4. A <u>gentleman</u> is kind to other people.	_____	_____
5. A <u>fact</u> is something that can't be proven.	_____	_____
6. <u>Honesty</u> is something to eat at breakfast.	_____	_____

Check your answers with the key on page 71.

Ready to Go

PREPARATION

Key Words

astronaut   (as´trə nôt)   a person who makes rocket flights into outer space
> *Peter hopes to become an <u>astronaut</u> someday.*

check   (chek)   to examine to find out if something is right or as it should be
> *Please <u>check</u> the answers on your math homework.*

guest   (gest)   a visitor
> *Please be my <u>guest</u> for dinner on Tuesday.*

locate   (lō´kāt)   find
> *If you <u>locate</u> my keys, please let me know.*

overhead   (ō´vər hed´)   above one's head
> *Make sure to turn off the <u>overhead</u> light before you leave.*

praise   (prāz)   to say good things about; give a good opinion of
> *If you <u>praise</u> a puppy, it may behave better.*

Ready to Go

Necessary Words

capsule (kap´sl)   the enclosed part of a space ship that holds the crew
The space <u>capsule</u> landed safely in the ocean.

chemical (kem´ə kl)   a substance that is made by or used in a chemical process
What <u>chemical</u> did we use to make the candy hard?

entrance (en´trəns)   a door, gate or other opening
Amy, please wipe your feet at the back door <u>entrance</u>.

include (in klüd´)   to take in as part of a whole; contain
Make sure to <u>include</u> us in the card game.

knights (nītz)   soldiers in the Middle Ages who were given a military rank of honor after training
The <u>knights</u> of King Arthur's Round Table are very well known.

portholes (pôrt´hōlz)   small windows in a ship's side for letting in light or air
We saw the island from our <u>portholes</u> on the ship.

Places

Rocky Mountains   is a mountain system in western North America.
It stretches from New Mexico to Alaska.

Ready to Go

"We'll be like kings up there on the moon," spoke Ardan.

Preview: 1. Read the name of the story.
                2. Look at the picture.
                3. Read the sentence under the picture.
                4. Read the first two paragraphs of the story.
                5. Then answer the following question.

You learned from your preview that Ardan wanted to change the capsule's

___a. design.
___b. color.
___c. shape.
___d. height.

Turn to the Comprehension Check on page 58 for the right answer.

Now read the story.

Read to find out how everyone prepared for the big day.

56

Ready to Go

The cannon that would shoot three men to the moon had been finished. But Michel Ardan, the artist and astronaut, wanted some changes made to the space capsule's design. He wanted to have more room overhead. It was a small capsule. He felt cramped inside. He felt like a squirrel in a cage. He got in touch with the company who built the capsule, and asked them to make a few changes. They said they would check the design and make the changes.

Ardan, Barbicane and Captain Nicholl were the three astronauts. They waited for all to be ready. The huge silver capsule sparkled in the sunlight.

"I almost expect to see knights of old, dressed in heavy metal armor, to come out of it!" said Ardan. "We'll be like kings up there on the moon," he continued. "With guns, we will be able to hold off enemies on the moon...if there are any."

Do you like the capsule?" Barbicane asked.

"Yes, of course," answered Ardan. "But I do wish we could decorate it more...maybe with flames shooting across the sides."

"What for?" asked Barbicane, surprised.

"I just feel that we should always put art into everything we do," answered Ardan. "But I won't decorate it without your okay. But we could sure use some nice things *inside*."

"You may arrange the inside any way you like," said Barbicane.

"Have you made a design to help soften our first crash landing on the moon?" Ardan asked, changing the subject.

"Yes. The bottom of the capsule will be filled with three feet of water. A wooden top will fit tightly over this. The water will help soften our moon landing," Barbicane explained.

"Amazing!" said Ardan. His voice was filled with praise.

The capsule was nine feet around and twelve feet high. It was entered through a hole in the top. They would locate the seal for the entrance on the inside.

"But how will we see *outside* the capsule?" Ardan and Nicholl thought to themselves.

As if reading their thoughts, Barbicane said, "We will be able to watch the earth as we leave it. We will view the outside through portholes made of special glass; one porthole hidden on each side of the capsule, and one overhead."

"And we'll see the moon as we get close!" exclaimed Ardan.

Food and water supplies were in solid containers. A special container stored gas for fire and light. There was enough gas to heat and light the capsule for six days.

And about the air? The air in the capsule would not be enough for three men to share for four days. The answer was simple. They would have to make *new* air. There was a chemical process that would let them make air they had already breathed, like new.

It was all very exciting. J.T. Maston said, "Since I am not going with you, please let me be a guest in the capsule for a time before you leave!"

Everyone agreed that this would be okay. He was given food, water, and enough chemicals to make new air for six days. He checked the items on his list. He was ready!

On November 12, at six o'clock in the morning, Maston was in the capsule. He sealed it himself from the inside.

What happened inside the capsule? Well, no one knows for sure. But six days later, at six o'clock, the cover was taken off the capsule.

"Hello!" came a voice from inside.

Maston came out of the capsule. Everyone stared at him, their mouths open. Maston had gained some weight!

Barbicane was excited when the huge telescope the Gun Club had ordered was finished. It was one of the last jobs to be done. The Gun Club members wanted to be able to see the capsule in space and on the moon. The telescope was 280-feet long! A high mountain had to be chosen to set it upon. It was decided that the Rocky Mountains would be best.

It was now just days before the capsule was to leave. Barbicane still worried about how the cannon would be lit. It was a dangerous process. He chose his best workers to light the cannon. He made sure that the huge amount of gunpowder needed was brought in a little at a time. That way, it would not be all in one place until the day of the launch. He wanted every part of this project to be safe for everyone. The town praised him for his care.

At last, it was time to place items in the capsule for the trip. Two guests would be on board in the form of two dogs. Barbicane made sure they had a map of the moon, and thermometers and telescopes aboard. They also took three shotguns, three rifles, and lots of bullets.

"There may be men or animals who won't like us visiting," said Ardan. "We must be prepared for anything."

Tools, such as picks, hammers and saws were also included. Seeds were brought in case they were able to plant food.

"Will we have *enough* food?" asked Nicholl, looking fearful.

"Well, the cannon will still be on earth, won't it?" asked Ardan.

"Of course," said Nicholl.

"Then why can't our friends on earth send us food once a year?"

"What a wonderful idea!" said Nicholl.

And finally, the time had come. The cannon was brought to the top of a big hill. Everything was now in place for the big day.

Ready to Go

Preview Answer:

a. design.

COMPREHENSION CHECK

Choose the best answer.

1. Michel Ardan felt the space capsule was
   _____a. too small inside.
   _____b. too big inside.
   _____c. too ugly inside.
   _____d. too hot inside.

2. The company that made the capsule said
   _____a. it was too late to change its design.
   _____b. it was too early to change the design.
   _____c. they had no time to change the design.
   _____d. they would check the design and change it.

3. Why do you think Ardan wanted to decorate the space capsule?
   _____a. It wasn't pretty.
   _____b. It was too plain.
   _____c. He was an artist by trade.
   _____d. He wanted to be comfortable.

4. The capsule was filled with three feet of water
   _____a. in case the astronauts got thirsty.
   _____b. to soften their moon landing.
   _____c. to wash their clothes.
   _____d. to wash their dishes.

5. How would the astronauts watch the earth as they left it?
   _____a. Through telescopes
   _____b. Through special glasses
   _____c. Through a special tube
   _____d. Through portholes made with special glass

6. Using a chemical process the astronauts would make
   _____a. new air to breathe.
   _____b. great-tasting food to eat.
   _____c. clean drinking water.
   _____d. new space suits.

7. J.T. Maston spent six days inside the space capsule. When he came out, what was different about him?
   _____a. He had grown old.
   _____b. His hair was very long.
   _____c. He had put on a few pounds.
   _____d. He was very thin.

8. Barbicane had taken great care to make sure that
   _____a. the capsule would return to earth.
   _____b. the project would be safe for everyone.
   _____c. all their weapons were in good working order.
   _____d. they packed enough food.

9. Another name for this story could be
   _____a. "New Air to Breathe."
   _____b. "Preparing for the Big Day."
   _____c. "Rifles and Bullets."
   _____d. "The Longest Telescope."

10. This story is mainly about
    _____a. how everyone prepared for the first space flight.
    _____b. how everyone prepared food for the journey.
    _____c. how the astronauts would breathe in space.
    _____d. how Ardan arranged the inside of the space capsule.

Check your answers with the key on page 67.

This page may be reproduced for classroom use.

Ready to Go

VOCABULARY CHECK

astronaut	check	guest	locate	overhead	praise

I. Sentences to Finish

Fill in the blank in each sentence with the correct key word from the box above.

1. Dad will _____ the tires to see if they need air.

2. Aunt Marie will be our house _____ this summer.

3. Dan's teacher did nothing but _____ his work.

4. That plant hanging _____ should be brought down and watered.

5. The _____ will return to earth in three days.

6. Marge tried to _____ her street on the map.

II. Matching

Unscramble the group of letters to spell out the key words. Match the key words in Column A with their meanings in Column B.

Column A

1. ispare _____

2. auntrosta _____

3. khecc _____

4. stuge _____

5. dorheave _____

6. coatel _____

Column B

a. above one's head

b. examine to find out if something is right

c. a person who makes rocket flights into outer space

d. to say good things about

e. to find

f. a visitor

Check your answers with the key on page 71

This page may be reproduced for classroom use.

59

Ready! Set! Fire!

PREPARATION

Key Words

nuisance	(nü´sns)	a thing or person that causes trouble or bother *My little brother is a big <u>nuisance</u>.*
orbit	(ôr´bit)	the path of a heavenly body or man-made craft as it revolves around another heavenly body *The spaceship planned to <u>orbit</u> the planet for two days.*
solve	(solv)	to find the answer to; to clear up *I hope my mom can help me <u>solve</u> this problem.*
spent	(spent)	passed *Billy and Tim <u>spent</u> the afternoon fishing.*
upset	(up´set´)	greatly disturbed *Amy was <u>upset</u> that her kitten ran away.*
urge	(ėrj)	to plead with in a strong way to do something *I <u>urge</u> you never to drink and drive.*

Ready! Set! Fire!

Necessary Words

anthem   (an´thəm)   song of praise, such as The Star Spangled Banner
> *Each morning our class stands and sings our national <u>anthem</u>.*

countdown   (kount´doun´)   the act of counting backward to zero to show how much time is left until the start of an event
> *The <u>countdown</u> for the rocket's take-off has just begun.*

gravity   (grav´ə tē)   the natural force that draws objects toward the center of the earth. Gravity causes objects to have weight.
> *Have you heard that a scientist named Newton discovered how <u>gravity</u> works?*

meteor   (mē´tē ər)   a shooting star; a mass of stone or metal that comes toward the earth from outer space
> *We watched the <u>meteor</u> glow in the night sky.*

national   (nash´ən l)   having to do with the nation as a whole
> *The brave soldier became a <u>national</u> hero.*

switch   (swich)   a device which opens or closes a circuit, like a light switch
> *Please turn the light <u>switch</u> off when you leave the room.*

Ready! Set! Fire!

The day of the launch had finally arrived. So many people had gathered to watch the big event.

Preview: 1. Read the name of the story.
2. Look at the picture.
3. Read the sentences under the picture.
4. Read the first three paragraphs of the story.
5. Then answer the following question.

You learned from your preview that the launch took place in

___a. December.
___b. November.
___c. January.
___d. October.

Turn to the Comprehension Check on page 64 for the right answer.

Now read the story.

Read to find out what would become of the astronauts.

Ready! Set! Fire!

The exciting day had finally arrived! The space capsule would make its way to the moon. Three daring men would be on board.

The sun shone brightly on this cool December day. Many people had spent the night without sleep because they were nervous about the big event. Would the capsule really reach the moon? No one could say. But Michel Ardan wasn't worried. He had spent a quiet night, sleeping like a baby.

Since sunrise, a large crowd of people began to gather near the hill where the event was to take place. People had come from all over the world to watch.

By seven o'clock that evening, the crowd had become quite large. When the moon had risen, shining brightly, the eager crowd began to shout words of cheer. It was almost time.

The three astronauts arrived. Addressing the crowd, Michel Ardan said, "We are ready to make our way into space!" The crowd roared again, as they waved to the crew.

"Thank you all for coming," added Barbicane. He was pleased at the number of people who supported their efforts.

Captain Nicholl, the third astronaut, was unusually quiet. He looked at the crowd with tears of joy in his eyes. He, like Barbicane, was pleased that so many had come to see them off. But he was upset that he might never see any of them again.

Just then, a band began to play the national anthem.

"You are heroes!" the crowd shouted. They yelled so loud that the music being played could hardly be heard. The excitement seemed to grow with every passing moment.

Then all became quiet, as the Frenchman and the two Americans entered the area where the cannon was located.

"Thank you all," said Ardan. "We'll bring you back some cheese from the moon---if there is any to be found," he joked. The crowd laughed loudly at his sense of humor.

The three astronauts stepped into a big, wire cage. Then the door closed.

"Lower us down!" Barbicane ordered.

Once again, the crowd fell silent. All except for Barbicane's good friend J.T. Maston.

"Why don't I come with you!" he shouted. "There's still time!"

"No, my friend," said Barbicane gently, from inside the cage. "It is too late now!"

"I urge you to think again!" yelled Maston.

Maston was becoming a bit of a nuisance. But Barbicane did not get angry. He had only kind words for his friend. "Thank you for your friendship, Maston," said Barbicane, a tear shining in his eye.

Now it was time. A great sadness came over the crowd as the cage was lowered down into the entrance of the cannon. For now the people were not able to see the three men enter the capsule. They could only listen. They could hear the final bolt fasten as it was turned. The men were now sealed inside the space capsule.

The moon shone and the stars glittered, while the crowd, so full of fear and excitement, could hardly breathe!

As the countdown began, the crowd joined in.

"Ten! Nine! Eight! Seven!

Would it work?

"Three! Two! One! Fire!" The switch was pressed and a spark went down to light the cannon.

A loud noise came from below that was louder than any sound ever heard before. The ground shook like an earthquake, as smoke and fire shot out of the ground. Only a few people saw the capsule shoot into the air. It had happened so fast!

All of Florida became as light as day from the fire's great light. Later, it was reported that the fire had been seen from other places far away. One ship's captain claimed he saw a meteor over the ocean that night! Could it have been the space capsule?

The crowd had been urged to stand far back when the cannon was fired, but few had listened. Many people were hurt from the blast, while others became deaf for awhile from the noise.

"Look at those trees!" shouted a man, pointing to what was left of them. The trees around the launch area had been destroyed during the blast; all that remained were burning, smoking sticks!

"It looks like a mighty storm has passed through here!" shouted another man.

And trees were not the only things destroyed during the blast. Some houses, not far from the launch area, had been uprooted. And a tropical storm had formed in the ocean, caused by the smoke and wind from the launch.

"Three cheers for our brave heroes!" shouted the crowd, as they waited to see what would happen next. They looked up in the sky, but they could not see the capsule, as there was still too much smoke. Maybe tomorrow.

But the next day was cloudy. And the next day. And the day after that. This bad weather was such a nuisance. Not even the men looking through the telescope on the mountain could see!

The three men had left on December 1. If all went well, they would arrive on the moon on December 4. But still, no one could see. People were quite upset about this.

"Where can they be?" cried Maston. He was worried about his friend.

All of a sudden, a tropical storm came and blew the clouds away.

The man in charge of the telescope gave the following report:

THE SPACE CAPSULE, SHOT FROM THE CANNON ON DECEMBER 1, HAS BEEN SEEN! IT HAS NOT REACHED THE MOON JUST YET. IT IS MAKING AN ORBIT AROUND THE MOON. TWO THINGS MAY HAPPEN - THE MOON'S GRAVITY MAY PULL THE CAPSULE DOWN TO THE MOON, OR THE CAPSULE MAY BE HELD IN ORBIT AROUND THE MOON FOREVER!

These three astronauts had enough chemicals to make new air for only two months. And they had enough food to last one year. But what then? Would these brave men just die up there in space? Could anyone on earth solve the problems these men would face, in so short a time?

Barbicane, Ardan, and Nicholl had asked themselves these very questions. And they could come up with no answers. But they were willing to risk their lives for the future of Man.

Ready! Set! Fire!

COMPREHENSION CHECK

Choose the best answer.

1. Everyone was nervous about the big event except for
   _____a. J.T. Maston.
   _____b. Barbicane.
   _____c. Michel Ardan.
   _____d. Captain Nicholl.

2. The launch took place
   _____a. in the evening.
   _____b. in the early morning.
   _____c. in the middle of the night.
   _____d. in the middle of the afternoon.

3. When Barbicane saw all the people that had come to see them off,
   _____a. he became angry.
   _____b. he became upset.
   _____c. he began to cry.
   _____d. he was pleased.

4. Captain Nicholl worried that he and the other astronauts
   _____a. were becoming heroes.
   _____b. would run into strange life forms on the moon.
   _____c. would end up on a different planet.
   _____d. might never return to the earth.

5. J.T. Maston was afraid that
   _____a. he might never see Barbicane again.
   _____b. Barbicane was not healthy enough to make the trip.
   _____c. Barbicane no longer wanted Maston as a friend.
   _____d. bad weather would cause the capsule to crash.

6. The launch caused a blast that
   _____a. killed everyone standing near the launch area.
   _____b. destroyed trees and homes near the launch area.
   _____c. destroyed the space capsule, killing the astronauts.
   _____d. destroyed the cannon.

7. Because of bad weather, the capsule was not sighted for
   _____a. several days.
   _____b. several hours.
   _____c. several weeks.
   _____d. several months.

8. The astronauts had enough food to last one year, and enough air to last
   _____a. one month.
   _____b. two months.
   _____c. six months.
   _____d. ten months.

9. Another name for this story could be
   _____a. "Lost in Space."
   _____b. "A Cool December Day."
   _____c. "A Tropical Storm Hits Florida."
   _____d. "First Flight Into Space."

10. This story is mainly about
    _____a. three brave men who risked their lives for the future of Man.
    _____b. three men who would solve the world's problems.
    _____c. three men who went to the moon looking for cheese.
    _____d. three men who became lost in space.

Check your answers with the key on page 67.

Ready! Set! Fire!

VOCABULARY CHECK

nuisance	orbit	solve	spent	upset	urge

I. Sentences to Finish
Fill in the blank in each sentence with the correct key word from the box above.

1. The stray dogs in our neighborhood are becoming a _____ .

2. I _____ you to listen to your doctor and stay in bed.

3. The moon will _____ the earth once every 29 1/2 days.

4. Mike _____ many days working on his science project.

5. Joe and Bill worked hard to _____ the problem together.

6. Mother was _____ with me for telling a lie.

II. Matching
Write the letter of the correct meaning from Column B next to the key word in Column A.

Column A	Column B
_____1. nuisance	a. to find the answer to; to clear up
_____2. orbit	b. to plead with in a strong way to do something
_____3. solve	c. a thing or person that causes trouble or bother
_____4. spent	d. passed
_____5. upset	e. the path of a heavenly body or man-made craft as it revolves around another heavenly body
_____6. urge	f. greatly disturbed

Check your answers with the key on page 72.

This page may be reproduced for classroom use.

NOTES

NOTES

COMPREHENSION CHECK ANSWER KEY
Lessons CTR D-61 to CTR D-70

LESSON NUMBER	1	2	3	4	5	6	7	8	9	10	PAGE NUMBER
CTR D-61	b	b	d	a	c	(d)	a	a	△d	□b	10
CTR D-62	c	b	c	d	(a)	(b)	d	b	△c	□a	16
CTR D-63	(c)	c	a	d	a	d	b	c	△a	□d	22
CTR D-64	(d)	c	a	b	d	d	a	(a)	△b	□d	28
CTR D-65	d	d	(a)	(b)	c	a	a	b	△c	□a	34
CTR D-66	b	(c)	a	d	b	d	a	c	△c	□a	40
CTR D-67	a	(d)	(b)	c	c	a	b	(a)	△b	□a	46
CTR D-68	d	(a)	(b)	c	a	c	a	b	△c	□d	52
CTR D-69	a	d	(c)	b	d	a	c	b	△b	□a	58
CTR D-70	c	a	d	(d)	(a)	b	a	b	△d	□a	64

○ = Inference (not said straight out, but you know from what is said)

△ = Another name for the story

□ = Main idea of the story

NOTES

VOCABULARY CHECK ANSWER KEY
Lessons CTR D-61 to CTR D-70

61   THE GUN CLUB   11

I. 1. colonel   *II.* 1. c
      2. insist   2. d
      3. succeed   3. f
      4. weary   4. b
      5. period   5. a
      6. action   6. e

62   THE PLAN   17

I. 1. celebrate   *II.*
      2. pride
      3. preparation
      4. national
      5. distant
      6. planet

```
                    ²D
              ¹P  R  I  D  E
              R     S
              E     T
              ²P  L  A  N  E  T
              A     N
              R     T     ³C
              A           E
        ³N  A  T  I  O  N  A  L
              I           E
              O           B
              N           R
                          A
                          T
                          E
```

63   THE OCTOBER MEETING   23

      1. problem
      2. October
      3. rocket
      4. support
      5. chosen
      6. design

VOCABULARY CHECK ANSWER KEY
Lessons CTR D-61 to CTR D-70

64   THE BET   **29**

I. 1. bet   *II.* 1. f
      2. expensive   2. c
      3. powder   3. a
      4. demand   4. b
      5. immediately   5. d
      6. length   6. e

65   OFF TO FLORIDA   **35**

I. 1. arrangement   *II.*
      2. degree
      3. tropical
      4. alligator
      5. climate
      6. zero

U	A	W	E	L	E	T	R	O
T	R	O	P	I	C	A	L	D
R	R	C	X	S	L	L	Z	E
O	A	L	C	E	I	L	E	G
P	N	I	O	M	M	I	R	R
A	G	M	L	P	A	G	A	X
R	E	A	D	P	T	A	L	G
R	M	A	F	N	E	T	L	G
A	E	L	Z	E	R	O	Q	R
N	N	L	D	E	G	R	E	E
G	T	Z	E	R	T	R	O	D

66   A MESSAGE TO BARBICANE   **41**

I. 1. impatient   *II.* 1. impatient, b
      2. December   2. disgrace, c
      3. disgrace   3. accept, d
      4. accept   4. date, e
      5. examination   5. examination, f
      6. date   6. December, a

VOCABULARY CHECK ANSWER KEY
Lessons CTR D-61 to CTR D-70

LESSON NUMBER		PAGE NUMBER
67	**MICHEL ARDAN ARRIVES**	47

1. champion
2. flight
3. accent
4. artist
5. news
6. crazy

68	**THE QUARREL**	53

I.
1. fact
2. mention
3. quarrel
4. hotel
5. honesty
6. gentleman

II.
1. True
2. False
3. False
4. True
5. False
6. False

69	**READY TO GO**	59

I.
1. check
2. quest
3. praise
4. overhead
5. astronaut
6. locate

II.
1. praise, d
2. astronaut, c
3. check, b
4. guest, f
5. overhead, a
6. locate, e

LESSON NUMBER

PAGE NUMBER

70   **READY! SET! FIRE!**   **65**

I.
1. nuisance
2. urge
3. orbit
4. spent
5. solve
6. upset

II.
1. c
2. e
3. a
4. d
5. f
6. b